Polar Bears of Churchill
Second Edition

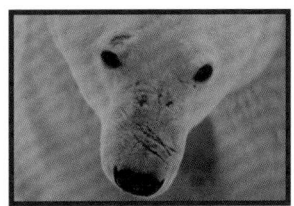

Special Thanks to:
Keith & Gail Eliasson, Carmen Spiech, Dave Pancoe,
Robert & Carolyn Buchanan, Kevin Burke Jr., Dr. Nick Lunn,
Joanne Simerson, Diana Weinhardt, John Bykerk

Polar Bears of Churchill
© 2006 - Kelsey Eliasson

All rights are reserved. The use of any part of this publication reproduced, transmitted in any form or by any means, electronic, mechanical, photocopying, recording or otherwise, or stored in a retrieval system, without the prior consent of the publisher, except in the case of brief quotations embodied in critical articles and reviews, is an infringement of copyright law.

ISBN 0-9780757-0-6

Published by Munck's Cafe
P.O. Box 123 - Churchill, Manitoba, Canada - R0B 0E0
www.polarbearalley.com

Printed and bound in Canada by Friesens Corporation - Altona, Manitoba, Canada

Credits:
Photographs on pages 13, 15, 21, 28, 31, 39, 41 and 42
by Dave Pancoe of Northern Soul Wilderness Canoeing Adventures
www.northernsoul.ca

Photograph on page 40
by Robert and Carolyn Buchanan of Polar Bears International
www.polarbearsinternational.org

All other photographs and maps by Kelsey Eliasson.

Special thanks to Nick Lunn of the Canadian Wildlife Service
and Richard Romaniuk of Manitoba Conservation for original interviews
that were used as source material for parts of this book.

Thanks to M. Hebert for the use of his image as 'buggy driver' on page 24 .

Cover Photo features Dancer, a long-time friend of Churchill's bear season

Table of Contents

Welcome to Bear Country	1
Summer on Land	5
Waiting for the Ice	9
Map of Wapusk National Park	11
Bear Season	15
Map of Tundra Trails	17
Bear Behaviour	21
Playfighting	25
Out on the Bay	29
Spring Hunt	33
Mothers and Cubs	37
Polar Bear Alert	43
Living With Bears	45
Polar Bear Research	47
The Future	49
Polar Bear Who's Who	51
Quick Reference	53
Physical Adaptations	55
Suggested Reading	57
Bibliography	57
Acknowledgements	58
Map of Manitoba	61

Welcome to Bear Country

There are approximately 1000 polar bears in the Western Hudson Bay population. It is one of the few polar bear populations that become landlocked for part of the year. As the ice breaks up in late July, these bears come ashore to summer inland or along the coast. They are generally spread out along the shore of Hudson Bay from Cape Tatnam near the Ontario border to the community of Churchill, Manitoba.

By early October, many bears begin to congregate along Cape Churchill. The Cape is a north-facing shelf jutting fifty kilometers (thirty miles) out into Hudson Bay. Prevailing north-western winds and the counter-clockwise current of Hudson Bay push the growing ice onto this landmass. This, combined with the massive freshwater outflow from rivers to the north, result in the ice forming earlier along the northwest coast of Hudson Bay.

This attracts many polar bears anticipating the return of their hunting grounds. Most years, enough ice has formed along the coast by mid-November and Churchill's bears have once again returned to their hunting grounds. It is the six week window leading up to this that has made Churchill, Manitoba an international tourist destination. For over twenty five years, people have been venturing out on tundra vehicles to view this gathering of polar bears. Many people have had the unique opportunity to view polar bears up close and in the wild – usually from the safety of a giant tin can on wheels!

Of course, by December, Churchill is quiet once again; bears and tourists have returned to their stomping grounds and frozen tumbleweeds virtually roll down the street. While tourists are spread out over the globe, the bears roam the western half of Hudson Bay. Through the heart of winter, they wait at seal breathing holes, wait out blizzards and basically wait for spring.

It is not until spring that the real action starts. Warmer temperatures mean that consistent leads or openings in the ice are found in western Hudson Bay. This brings increased access to seals and their birthing dens. For these three or four months, polar bears feast on a wealth of newborn and inexperienced ringed seals. Of course, much like tourist season, spring is over all too soon and the bears are back on land to begin waiting once again.

Bear Facts:
Hudson Bay and Beyond

- Polar bears inhabit the circumpolar regions around the north pole, including northern Russia, the Canadian Arctic, the coast of Alaska, Greenland (Denmark) and Norway's Spitzbergen Island. 25,000-30,000 polar bears are thought to exist worldwide with Canada home to around 15,000 of these animals.

- They spend the vast majority of their lives on sea ice with only a few populations spending significant time on land. The exception being pregnant females who more commonly venture onto land to prepare their maternity dens.

- One of the most effectively managed arctic species, polar bears are not endangered. However, as a top predator, they are considered high risk to environmental change, including pollution, climate change and human impact, such as overhunting.

- There are twenty partially discrete polar bear populations known to exist. Three of these populations frequent Hudson Bay – western Hudson Bay (extending from the Manitoba/Ontario border to Chesterfield Inlet, Nunavut), southern Hudson Bay (James Bay) and Foxe Basin (at the northwestern edge of the bay).

- This population is one of the most accessible in the world. In fact, much of our knowledge of polar bear biology and behaviour comes from research conducted in the Churchill area. The Canadian Wildlife Service has over thirty years of continuous research data about Churchill's polar bears, one of the longest research programs in existence.

- Based on CWS research, the breakup of Hudson Bay is thought to occur about 2.5 weeks earlier than in the early 1980s. This leaves the bears less time on the ice during their prime hunting season (April through July) and an estimated 22kgs (50lbs) lighter.

Summer on Land

The ice usually lasts well into summer but, by the end of July, the bears are back on shore. As wind and ocean currents push the dwindling ice floes down the coast, the polar bears begin to swim ashore. This begins a minimum three month 'fast' where the bears will not have access to their main food source.

Pregnant females and mothers with cubs come ashore first. They leave the ice as it passes Wapusk National Park and the maternity denning area. This can be up to two weeks prior to the final breakup, occurring near Cape Tatnam and the Manitoba/Ontario border.

They do this for several reasons. One, females are fairly site specific, many of them return to an area within forty kilometres (25 miles) of their birthing den. Also, it seems the extra seals are just not worth the extra distance. It is believed that bears kill a seal, on average, every five days. The energy acquired from another couple seals are not worth another couple hundred kilometre walk back to the denning area.

It is the large males that ride the dwindling ice to the bitter end, coming ashore in the southwest corner of Hudson Bay. From here, they begin their plodding migration back to the beach ridges of Cape Churchill.

Along the way, they gather along the spits and gravel ridges along the coast, basking in the cool winds coming off the water. While looks may be deceiving, the living is not easy in the summer time. These large males are merely seeking temporary relief from temperatures that can reach over 30C (90F) and biting insects that can be found in unreasonable and unrelenting proportions.

Uncommon in most polar bear populations, the largest males may gather in groups of up to fifteen but usually ranging from two to six bears. How these groupings fit in to the complicated hierarchy of polar bears remains to be seen. Polar Bears International is working with Parks Canada to establish remote control cameras at Cape Churchill, within Wapusk National Park, as a means of further, non-intrusive research into the bears' summer home.

Bear Facts:
In The Summertime

- Adult males congregate along the coastal regions and gravel spits. Several of these spits near Churchill have been designated as polar bear resting areas, including sections of Eskimo Point and Gordon Point.

- Females (pregnant or not) and some males (definitely not pregnant) spend time in earthen dens during the summer…it is cooler there and there are less bugs.

- April through July are the most productive hunting months for Churchill's bears. Young seals are high in fat and not that experienced with predators. Therefore, the timing of breakup is critical for polar bears. If the ice breaks up even a week early, this may cost the bears up to 10kg (22lbs) in fat stores.

- After months of feeding, bears are very fat when they finally swim ashore. With up to 4" of blubber, the bears are quite buoyant. This makes swimming a lot easier but diving a little difficult; their rump bobbing up to the surface much like a cork - not a very strategic position!

- Once on land, bears spend the vast majority (70-90%) of their time simply resting. Given the right conditions, however, they forage on berries, sedges, grasses, kelp, snowmobile seats and almost anything else.

- Polar bears are highly intelligent and adaptable. Bears have been seen hunting caribou, beluga whales, snowy owls, eider ducks… well, you get the picture. Along the Seal River, a polar bear was observed lunging onto the backs of passing beluga whales.

- During the summer and in times of food shortage, polar bears can enter a state of walking hibernation. They reduce their metabolism, lowering energy demands to conserve their fat stores.

Waiting for the Ice

By mid-October, cooler temperatures bring a change in the bears. Restless, sensing a change in the season, many return to Churchill and gather along the coast in eager anticipation of the coming ice. Once here, some pace along the coast, roll around the willows, graze on some kelp or spar with a friend.

Most, however, pass the time in a 'day bed'. A 'day bed' is simply a good resting spot, comfortable and sheltered. Preferred locations include willow thickets along the shallow tundra ponds and the deep kelp beds on the coast. There are certain 'day beds' along Cape Churchill that are used day after day, often year after year.

Resting is not without its complications. Larger, or simply more aggressive bears, often approach and displace sleeping bears. Once 'victorious', however, they may occupy the bed for only a short time.

Many times, the displaced bear will return, after walking a large, cautionary circle back to its original resting area. Once here, it is again, time to rest and wait.

Waiting pays off. With each succeeding tide, a little more ice clings to the shore. Each day, the ice reaches out a little further into the bay. And each day, the bears test the ice more and more.

Though considered a marine mammal, bears still prefer not to get wet in cold temperatures. Walking on newly formed ice, polar bears often spread all four legs further and further apart until their belly almost touches the ice. Their large paws distribute their weight very effectively, allowing them to walk on ice that would not support the weight of a person…and especially not the weight of a tundra vehicle.

Alternately, they may test the strength of the new ice as they progress, giving a little pump with their front paws. As the shore ice builds so does the bears' anticipation. By season's end, many bears will be seen wandering along the ice's edge, far out onto the bay.

Bear Facts:
Polar Bear Dens and Wapusk National Park

While most bears gather along the coast, some have other plans. Pregnant females remain inland in maternity dens in the heart of Wapusk National Park. Established in 1996, Wapusk National Park covers 11,475 square kilometres of the Hudson Bay lowlands.

Both Wapusk National Park and the surrounding Churchill Wildlife Management Area (established in 1978) protect one of the largest polar bear maternity denning areas in the world. This area supports approximately 100-150 denning females each year and produce on average 200-300 cubs.

The dens are unique to the polar bears of Hudson Bay. Most polar bear populations use dens made of snow or a combination of earth and snow within about 16km (10 miles) of shore. However, the western Hudson Bay population travels an average of 30-50km (20-30 miles) and some over 100+km (60 miles) inland in search of suitable denning habitat.

Their needs are quite specific in the Churchill area. They pick spots that gather ample snow, usually the south facing shores of small lakes or creeks. On the lea side of the prevailing winds, they dig into large banks of peat, hollowing out a den in the permafrost about 2-3 metres (6-9') and one metre (3') high.

A layer of black spruce will be found on top of these denning sites, their intertwined root systems providing strength to the ceiling and security in the winter. Forest fires, however, can destroy this ceiling, rendering the den unusable. With most fires started by lightning in this area, the hotter, dryer summers associated with climate change present another potential threat to Churchill's bears. While most of these fires are contained by the many of tundra ponds, it is conceivable that one lightning strike could eliminate much of the suitable denning habitat for this population.

courtesy of Dave Pancoe
www.northernsoul.ca

Bear Facts:
The Ice Forms

Salt water becomes heavier as it freezes. This leaves a greasy soup of ice washing in and out with the tide, each wave leaving just a little more ice clinging to the shore. In Churchill, high tide returns every 12.5 hours and it does not take long for the shore ice to extend well out into the tidal zone.

As well, Hudson Bay's watershed extends west to the Canadian Rockies and south to Minnesota. This means that a tremendous amount of fresh water pours into the bay from several northern rivers. This inflow results in brackish water (a mix of salt and fresh water) along the coast and surface of Hudson Bay. Since freshwater begins to freeze at a higher temperature than salt water, this further contributes to the speed of freeze up.

All the while, the ice builds along the northwestern coast of Hudson Bay. Soon, the 'grease ice' forms into little ice floes called pancake ice. A strong north wind and consistently cold temperatures of -20C (-4F) or lower will push this ice together and pack it onto the coast of Cape Churchill.

Once these sheets have frozen together, it signals the bears' departure. They will venture out to hunt seals even with only a few kilometres of ice. As winter progresses, the ice continues to encroach eastward until the bay is completely frozen, usually occurring in early December.

Almost every year, initial freeze up occurs around mid-November. However, in both 1991 and 2002, conditions prevailed for an early freeze. The freeze up was so sudden in 1991 that the bears departed near Halloween night. In other years, winter takes its time – 1999 and 2003 saw the bears remain ashore well into December. While a late freezeup is not as critical to the bears' health as an early breakup, it does result in an extreme increase in polar bear occurrences within the community of Churchill.

Bear Season

Polar bear tours are primarily held in the Churchill Wildlife Management Area, a provincially managed zone 25 kilometres east of Churchill. It has traditionally been one of the areas in which polar bears gather each fall. It has also become an area where tundra vehicles filled with eager tourists gather each fall.

There are eighteen permits issued for use by tundra vehicles. Starting at a place called Halfway Point, the polar bear viewing trails stretch another ten kilometres east to Gordon Point and the location of the original tundra vehicle lodge.

Many of the tundra vehicle trails near Gordon Point were first used when it was a military training grounds. The United States military first moved into the Churchill area in 1943. Practically overnight, they set up a tent city in Hudson Square, right in the middle of town and eventually developed an entire military community near the present-day airport. In the early years, the Churchill area was primarily used for cold weather exercises to test both men and equipment. One of the few landmarks in the Wildlife Management Area is First Tower, a military observation tower, located near Gordon Lake. It is a holdover of the cold weather exercises held in this area. By the late sixties, the bulk of the military presence in Churchill had departed. With this decline in activity, polar bears began appearing in and around the community of Churchill.

Soon, a few local residents began offering polar bear watching tours on assorted off-road and track vehicles. This started a wildlife viewing industry that is now over twenty five years old. One of the more famous entrepreneurs was Len Smith, creator of the world famous Tundra Buggies®. These vehicles were first featured in the 1979 National Geographic special 'Polar Bear Alert'. Tundra vehicles based on his design are now the primary means of viewing polar bears.

On average, about 300 polar bears pass through or near this area each year. Bears that choose to stay, generally become acclimatized within only twenty four hours, gaining confidence and an ease amidst the tundra vehicles.

Bear Facts:
How To Drive a Tundra Vehicle

While most polar bears are quite comfortable around tundra vehicles, it is important to understand their behaviour. The main challenge for any tundra vehicle driver is to anticipate the bear's immediate behaviour. Often, a tundra vehicle can be positioned so that the bear's natural path leads to a closer viewing opportunity.

Also, never underestimate the curiosity of a polar bear. If you have enough patience, the bear will often get up and walk over to the vehicle, just to check things out.

If a bear is already moving, just park and wait for it. Of course, chances are it has something else on its mind already and probably will not stay around your vehicle for long.

When approaching a resting bear, try not to drive straight towards the bear. An angled approach is much less likely to be taken as 'aggressive'.

There are three behaviours to watch for while approaching a resting bear. They signal the bear's attitude towards the tundra vehicle. It is important to keep your hand on the ignition, ready to shut the engine down, as these three behaviours can occur over a few minutes or a few seconds.

First, watch for eye contact. Bears are extremely observant and will begin to watch potential threats without moving a muscle. Second, they may raise their head, lifting for a better view or nosing the air for an identifying scent. Finally, many bears will slightly move their paw if they are feeling uneasy. This signal at any time is a sign to stop immediately and let the bear decide matters from there.

Different bears have different ideas of personal space, some pass by Gordon Point completely, seen only as a distant speck; others walk or even climb right up on the vehicles, as evidenced by the shadow of a surprised photographer's head (mine!) on the bear pictured below.

Bear Behaviour

Living on the ice or tundra, there are no trees to climb or ready escape routes. Polar bears must be confident in their ability to identify potential threats. Interpreting their surroundings and bear behaviour will mean the difference between confrontation or companionship in bear season, and likely be the difference in terms of survival out on the ice.

Smell is their strongest sense. At least twenty times more sensitive than human's, it is usually their first indicator of a pending encounter. This sense, however, is highly dependent on weather conditions and wind direction. For this reason, bears stretch their long necks and contort their noses to 'read' the wind.

Polar bears have come to rely on body language as their primary means of communication. With so many bears in a relatively small area, 'bear season' is an excellent opportunity to observe their complex interactions. Body size is often used to establish dominance. Bears will often 'broadside', walking at almost a right angle to their opponent. Two bears circle each other, assessing the situation and their opponent.

A lowered head is, also, a common behaviour. It can indicate uncertainty, stress or aggression. A bear often stands with a lowered head and all four feet close together while assessing new situations.

Uncertainty is often accompanied by swaying either their head or their whole body back and forth. Stress will often induce a licking motion, with bears sticking out their black tongue possibly to aid in identifying a new scent. Aggression is signified by an extended upper lip and an exhalation of breath or a hissing sound.

Although generally silent, bears may accompany the nuances of body language with vocalizations. A low growl can signify a warning to other bears, often used when food is involved. Despite this warning, food may be shared between bears, given the proper etiquette and conditions. On the other hand, trying to share someone else's food is a good way for a young bear to get in big trouble. A loud roar displays outright anger and often signals an immediate charge.

With such an adaptable and intelligent animal, it is amazing to watch how uncertainty changes to comfort to aggression and back in a very short time span.

Bear Facts:
Teaching and Learning Behaviours

Mothers with cubs again present some of the most interesting moments in bear season. She is in almost constant communication with her cubs whether they are listening or not.

Presented by an uncertain situation or threatening bear, she often keeps her cubs behind her, leaving them sitting together until she has assessed the potential danger. Ever alert, she not only uses body language but may also smack her lips, huff and even growl at her cubs. Often, one sound from her and her otherwise carefree cubs come running to her side. Some mothers are very disciplined, keeping a 'tight leash' on their cubs, others let their young ones roam, sometimes even a little too far…

The cubs, for their part, watch their mother intently, often mimicking her behaviours and her movements. During 'bear season', cubs of older, confident bears, sometimes even team up to drive away other bears. With their front lip extended, they have been seen charging at bears well over 200kg (400lbs) heavier. Of course, it does not hurt that mom is standing right behind her cubs. While females stay away from males as a general rule, it is a rare male that will attack a mother defending her cubs. Most know, that it is a battle that they will not likely leave unscarred. However, with occasional cases of cannibalization recorded amongst bears, females usually choose discretion over valour.

Cubs will stay with their mother for two or three years learning how to hunt and how to survive. These first years are critical to these bears' life path. The female's actions and patterns will impact her cubs and their behaviours for much of their life. Studies have shown that cubs encountered near Churchill or at the former garbage dump site had a high percentage of returning in later life to become problem bears. Since females prefer to return to familiar areas, young females were more likely to return and bring successive generations to the site.

courtesy of Dave Pancoe
www.northernsoul.ca

Playfighting

One of the highlights of Churchill's polar bear season are the raucous playfights of the large male bears.

As the season progresses and the temperatures drop, the resident bears become more active and begin to playfight. Some spar and break off, others partner up, playing and resting together for a few days. Certain bears will spar with a wide variety of bears over the season or even throughout the day!

Fights usually start when one bear ambles over and signals his intent, with a lowered head or even a nudge or bite. The two bears then 'mouth'. Face to face, they open their jaws wide, moving and seemingly sizing each other up. Soon, the intensity builds. They wrestle, trying to wrap a massive paw around the other's neck. Inevitably, one, often both, will rise on his back haunches and lunge forward to shove or tackle his opponent.

There seems to be a fair amount of strategy. Each bear, especially the smaller one, waiting for the moment when his opponent is maybe a little off balance. In many of the playfights, one bear will be generally dominant, however, this hardly means that the fights are one-sided. The stronger bear often 'lets' the smaller bear compete, seemingly enjoying the thrill of the fight more than the victory. Fights are rarely serious with blood drawn only occasionally, usually when two bears are a little too evenly matched.

Playfighting is also common with cubs. Young bears will frolic and fight for hours on end, with the larger, usually male, cub dominating. Adult females with a single cub will also 'spar' with their offspring.

Subadult bears, three or four years old, may team up, likely to compete with larger bears for food and dominance. These partners may also be seen playfighting, albeit in slightly less dramatic bouts than the largest males. It is thought that some of these teams are siblings, recently separated from their mother. They may stay together to increase their chances of survival during the first full season on their own.

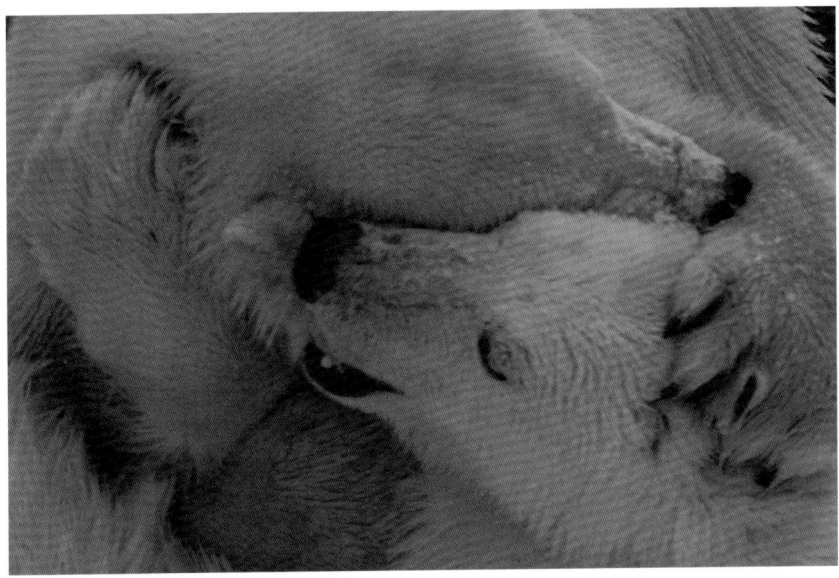

Bear Facts:
The Competition for Mates

With mating season half a year away, the playfighting in October and November seems to be just some good ol' rough and tumble fun. This fun, however, may also allow the bears to size up potential competition for mates.

During this playfighting, the polar bear's testosterone is amongst its lowest annual levels. This is not the case in spring. Male polar bears' testes begin to drop in mid-winter and they are ready to mate as early as March. Peak mating season occurs in late April through May and the competition is fierce. Driven by the scent produced during the female's estrous, males have been recorded tracking potential mates for over 100 kilometres (60 miles). Of course, other bears usually have the same idea...

The mating continues over several days, the duration of which the male must fend off spirited competitors. Vicious battles between large male bears often result in scars, wounds, and broken bones. An injured jaw or shoulder can mean the end for an otherwise healthy bear. Unable to hunt effectively or defend their food, it is a slow decline; making for a frustrated and dangerous bear.

Injured bears are not the only frustrated ones. Though sexually mature by three to five years of age, most male polar bears do not breed until close to ten years old. Most are unable to compete with the larger males and must simply bide their time.

This competition and ultimate dominance of the largest bears results in significant 'sexual dimorphism' (the size differences between males and females) among polar bears. Only the largest males are consistently successful in securing mates while most females reproduce regularly. This has created a genetic makeup where male polar bears are usually one and a half times larger than females. Voila, sexual dimorphism!

courtesy of Dave Pancoe
www.northernsoul.ca

Out on the Bay

By mid-November, ice covers much of Hudson Bay. Most of the bears, young and old, have returned to the ice, but their work has just begun. While seals are available, hunting is still difficult.

In order to survive these extreme climates polar bears have developed complex physical adaptations. By late October, the bears' undercoat gets much thicker, so thick that it gets very hard to find their skin through it. Researchers estimate that a bear's coat consists of almost ten thousand hairs per square inch by mid-winter. Obviously, their cold resistance is considerable.

This is not to say, however, that polar bears are completely resistant to the arctic winter. Strong winds and cold ambient air temperatures still affect them. The guard hairs keep a warm layer of air next to the skin and strong winds penetrate these hairs, undermining their insulative value. For this reason, they often wait out the winter storms, taking shelter on the lee side of snow banks and ice ridges. Sometimes, bears will stay motionless for days, only to rise and shake away a layer of snow as the storm breaks.

As well, water affects their ability to maintain heat. This affect is very noticeable during Churchill's bear season. Polar bears go to some incredible efforts to avoid getting wet! They will divert their path to avoid the many tundra ponds near Churchill. In fact, the bulk of visiting polar bears do not arrive in the Churchill area until many of the inland ponds have a fresh layer of ice.

However, the anticipation of winter is strong and testing ice is a common pass time during bear season, sometimes ending with the groan and crack of breaking ice and a very wet bear. On a warm day this is welcome, on cold days it is less than comfortable. Absorbing heat twenty five times faster than air, water can soak to the bear's skin and cools it quickly. To a large male with four inches of fat, this may not matter but to a younger, thinner bear, it could be fatal. To avoid this, their guard hairs are oily and shed water quickly. Emerging from the ocean or a partially frozen tundra pond, bears quickly shake excess water from their coat.

In a further adaptation to life on the ice, polar bears are almost completely furred, even much of their paws are covered. Their foot pads are also covered with little bumps. These bumps, or papillae, provide extra traction while traversing ice ridges on the rugged sea ice. Finally, their claws, short and strong, are also sharply curved; providing even greater ability to navigate the frozen ocean.

As with all arctic animals, their appendages, mainly their ears and tail, are smaller than other bears. This follows the idea that less surface area results in less heat loss. Polar bears emanate almost no heat, only their black noses and a wisp of breath showing up on infrared or heat sensitive cameras.

Bear Facts:
Walking Hibernation

Now, the ice bear is not really thrilled with the raging blizzards of mid-winter. Despite their thick layer of fat and woolly undercoat, polar bears are still susceptible to heat loss from strong winds and plummeting temperatures. Many bears will simply 'hunker down' and conserve energy through the coldest months.

As well, polar bears can enter in and out of their 'walking hibernation' at any time of the year. After seven to ten days without food their metabolic rate (heart beat, etc) will slow down allowing them to withstand prolonged periods of fasting. Essentially, it allows polar bears to survive periods of food deprivation that would be fatal to other mammals.

Spring Hunt

Spring is a time of plenty for Churchill's polar bears. Ringed seals, the main diet of polar bears, are giving birth on the sea ice in March and April. Since the majority of ringed seals caught by polar bears are one year old or less, this is as good a time as any to fatten up.

There are two main hunting strategies employed by polar bears: still-hunting and stalking. Still-hunting is by far the most common. The still-hunt amounts to a big chess game out on the the ice. Seals use a number of breathing holes, decreasing their chances of predation. The polar bear simply stakes out a seal breathing hole, lies down beside it, waits and hopes. The majority of still hunts last less than an hour but, that being said, polar bears are known for their patience and perseverance.

If a seal surfaces, the bear will either grab it with its powerful jaws or kill it with a crushing blow from its paw, dragging it from the water. Often, only the skin and fat of the seal is devoured. Highly digestable and high in fat and protein, it provides nutrition and hydration and is the mainstay of the polar bear diet. The other technique is stalking. With the warmer temperatures of spring, seals haul out near a breathing hole and bask on the ice; periodically sleeping and waking up to scan for threats then dozing off again. A polar bear will attempt to time its approach with the seal's sleep patterns. As the bear makes its slow approach, it freezes periodically, remaining motionless while the seal is awake. When the seal once again closes its eyes, the approach begins again. Once the bear is close enough, likely within 30 metres (100'), it makes its final charge. If the seal cannot slip back through its breathing hole in time, then that's all, folks.

Occasionally, seal kills occur during Churchill's bear season. Seals sleep in the water and may become stranded in the vast tidal zone along Cape Churchill. Once locked in a tidal pool or trapped on a boulder, they have to wait up to twelve hours for the water to return. This is a might stressful and probably fatal.

After a kill has been made, other bears will approach, nose in the air, jogging in a zig zag pattern to hone in on the scent. Successful hunters usually try to devour as much seal as quickly as possible but once more bears have arrived, they may even share their meal, assuming the proper etiquette has been shown . In the following days, the successful hunter will continue to venture out to the tidal zone or patrol the coast on a regular basis trying to repeat their feat; just another example of their incredible learning capacity.

Bear Facts:
Hunting Adaptations

Polar bears are opportunistic hunters. They have been recorded stalking caribou, raiding eider duck colonies, catching geese from underneath the water and even taking a passing swipe at a snowy owl, raven or snow bunting.

Individual bears can adapt hunting strategies in a wide variety of ways. One interesting adaptation is the ice floe impersonation. A polar bear will swim/float within striking distance of a seal or even beluga whale. Bears have been witnessed exhibiting this behaviour in the Churchill River!

During Churchill's bear season, you can watch bears learn how to hunt...tourists. In 2005, one bear, nicknamed Number One (pictured on page 20), learned to use the handle on the side of the Tundra Vehicles as added leverage to get just that much closer to a free lunch. Over the years, there have been bears who have learned to open doors, slide windows, climb on tires - luckily, we are too skinny for most bears to put forth that much effort.

Inuit hunters have told stories crediting bears with a variety of adaptations, including covering their black nose with their paw while stalking or even using large ice blocks to kill walrus. While these stories have not been scientifically confirmed, the bears' intelligence and resourcefulness should not be underestimated. Of course, I tend to take the word of people that used to hunt bears with a sharpened 3' long stick even if it has not been proven.

Anyone who has spent time around polar bears knows that they are always watching and learning and waiting. Often, they seemingly nonchalantly assess a situation and retreat, only to come back under cover of darkness and enact their plan. Regardless, it is quite clear that many bears learn after only one repetition. This combined with their curiousty makes life in polar bear country quite interesting.

Mothers and Cubs

The reproductive process of a female polar bear is one of the most incredible achievements of any animal on this planet. It begins as receptive females enter estrous (reproductive state) and mate out on the ice in late April or early May.

Mating lasts for several days and, during this time, the male must fend off several competitors, provided he has not steered the female to their own private spot! This prolonged period of mating may be an adaptation aimed at ensuring that the largest and most capable male bears are most likely to mate. This would, thereby, improve the likelihood of cub survival.

Testosterone is running highest at this time of year. While the male is quite gentle almost suave in his courtship, copulation is a different story, occasionally resulting in a broken bacculum (the polar bear's penis bone). Ouch!

Of course, if a male cannot fend off his competition for the duration of the process, cubs born in the same litter, may not necessarily have the same father.

While the egg has been fertilized by mid-May, the pregnancy does not begin for another four months. This is the result of an adaptation called delayed implantation. Unless the female has maintained a minimum weight of 300kg (660lbs) by September, the egg will simply be reabsorbed.

She needs these excess fat stores, as from mid-July through to the following February, she will have little or no access to food. During this time, she will move inland, prepare a maternity den, give birth, nurse her young and, in late winter, lead them to the coast. Once there, she must seek out seal birthing lairs and break into them, sometimes through one metre (3') of snow, to both feed herself and her cubs. Only then, does she begin two years of feeding, protecting and teaching her cubs.

Bear Facts:
Nursing

Witnessing a mother polar bear nursing her cubs is one of the best moments of any bear season. Female polar bears nurse their cubs for approximately two years. In the first months, their milk is rich in protein and comprised of over 30% fat content. While this fat content declines over time, the cubs grow quickly.

First year cubs, also known as COYs (Cubs of the Year), generally nurse for five or ten minutes every few hours. Often, they will start nudging their mother to signal their hunger. Some even vocalize their opinion with a loud, nagging bray.

Females nurse from a sitting position. In preparation, they will fix a day bed, either amidst the kelp or along the edge of a snowdrift. The cubs will sit and watch as mother digs and packs down her 'chair', not unlike the way a dog 'nests' before laying down. Once she settles into position, the cubs waste no time nestling into her lap to begin nursing.

Her movements become very fluid and very gentle. She nudges her young as they quietly coo and purr while suckling. Sometimes, she will lift her head, stretching her neck in an elegant curve. Eventually, she lays down on her side signaling the end of the session. Of course, if one cub, usually the male, gets a little too assertive, nursing can end abruptly, her gentleness quickly turning into a hard cuff, sending her cub rolling away!

It is extremely important for polar bear watchers to remain quiet and respectful during this rare opportunity. The female must feel comfortable through the entire process from preparation of the daybed to her final stretch; any distractions may make her nervous enough to get up and cut meal time short, leaving everybody, both tourists and cubs, more than a little disappointed.

Motherhood starts in mid-September with pregnant females nestled into an earthen maternity den and the three month pregnancy just beginning. Near Churchill, cubs are born in early to mid-December once the den has become covered and insulated by a layer of snow.

Less than one kilogram (2.2 lbs) at birth, they are blind, lightly furred and utterly helpless. While the den remains fairly comfortable, close to 0C (32F), up to thirty or forty degrees warmer than temperatures outside, she will also use her breath and body heat to keep her cubs warm.

Inside the den, the female does not eat or drink, her body absorbing its waste. From a normal rate of 70 beats per minute, her heart rate drops as low as eight beats per minute. It is in this state that she gives birth and even nurses. The cubs grow quickly, thriving on mother's high fat, high protein milk. Weighing around 9-14kg (20-30 lbs), they emerge from the den between late February and mid-March.

After spending a week or so acclimating to the temperatures and exercising, they begin the journey to the sea ice. With most dens 30-50km (20-30 miles) inland, this is no small feat for a little polar bear. Many do not make it. There seems to be less than a 50% chance of survival through the first year of life, overall. Naturally, first time mothers (about five years of age) lose the majority of their cubs while older, stronger, smarter females are much more successful in raising their young. The chances of survival for polar bear cubs increase with the age of the mother, generally up to about fifteen years of age.

Spring is a critical time of year for mothers and cubs. The females energy is taxed by milk production and the fact that she has not eaten for up to eight or nine months, one of the longest fasting periods for any mammal.

In this tender state, she must guide her cubs to the coast and the seal birthing lairs. As well, the polar bears of Churchill are one of the few populations with active predators, some cubs are taken by

the resident wolf population. The pack may work to separate the mother from one or both of her cubs.

Young mothers rarely succeed in this journey, some even abandon their cubs along the way. Older, more experienced bears, however, have a much better chance of success. They generally show an incredible bond with their young, exhibiting patience and care. Through deep snow or difficult terrain, a female may even let the cubs climb on her back, to rest as she carries them to the ice.

The incredible challenges associated with pregnancy and motherhood means that this group of bears are most likely to be negatively affected by the fluctuating weather and ice patterns associated with climate change. Remember, females need to maintain at least 200kg (440lbs) of fat reserves for their pregnancy to initiate. Without a good spring hunt, the egg will simply be reabsorbed. If this hunting season is reduced significantly, it could mean that overall cub production will be reduced to the point where it does not offset the mortality rate.

Polar Bear Alert

Churchill is built on some prime polar bear real estate. Each year, the bears' natural northward progression leads many of them to and through town! To manage this unique challenge, Churchill has its own Polar Bear Alert program.

This program began in 1967, when the Manitoba Department of Natural Resources decided to 'study polar bear occurrences to determine how many bears became problems annually' and by 1969, the first polar bear patrol was put into action in the Churchill area. Within a few years, the patrol started airlifting problem bears, primarily with funds provided by the International Fund for Animal Welfare. A variety of locations were tried with differing degrees of success. Eventually, relocation to the North River area, about 50 kilometres northwest of Churchill, proved to be the most successful. Relocation, simply continued the bear's natural progression northward.

However, by the mid-1970s, the situation had changed considerably. The Fort Churchill military base (near the present day airport) and several other smaller coastal communities were abandoned at that time. The reduced hunting pressures, both traditional and illegal, combined with the removal of the Fort Churchill dump, a definite bear attractant outside of town limits, resulted in a drastic increase in polar bear activity within the community of Churchill!

By 1976, 220 bear sightings were recorded in the Churchill area (up from only 76 in 1967). As well, the 65 problem bears in residential sites were the highest number on record.

As a result of concerns expressed by mayor and council at the time, a local Churchill Polar Bear Committee, consisting of Churchill residents, members of council and Provincial Wildlife Branch representatives, was established. By 1977, this committee submitted fourteen recommendations and urged the acquisition of Building D-20 at Fort Churchill as a temporary holding place. The facility, designed to hold up to 23 bears, opened in June 1980. With over 1,000 bears handled, the Polar Bear Alert program has worked very effectively at managing this human-bear overlap.

Living With Bears

Cabin life is always interesting in Churchill. Most times when you step out the door, it is accompanied by a quick check around for big, white rocks with sharp teeth! Bears have an uncanny ability to appear when you least expect them.

Most people who venture outside of Polar Bear Alert's regular patrol zone carry a shotgun for defence. These are usually loaded first with cracker shells - non-lethal shells loaded with black powder - and then with steel slugs as a second resort. Often, the loud bang associated with cracker shells is enough to move a bear away. If not, a cracker shell in their toe works pretty well. However, they learn very quickly and a 'crackered' bear will likely return later in the evening or at dawn to resume his investigations.

The best defence for people and cabins is a big dog that hates bears. It is a lot of fun to watch a good bear dog 'work' a bear. They dart in and out and circle around, barking and trying to bite that big ol' bear bum! Usually, excessive barking and cracker shells are a good combination to get the 'move along' message across to unwelcome visitors.

Nail boards, also called a 'Churchill welcome mat', are a good start for cabin owners. These are made with 3/4" plywood and a whole bunch of nails. For the most part, they are a good deterrent placed under or even attached to doors and windows. On the other hand, I have seen bears standing on nail boards and getting quite grumpy!

However, not much is going to stop a bear if it really sets its mind to something. The best description I have heard about a bear-struck cabin is that it is 'like someone picked up the cabin, turned it over, shook it and then put it back.' Bears have peeled off nails boards, chewed through walls, popped out windows (frames and all) and even broken through roofs. Once inside, they may tear apart one room and walk through another leaving it untouched!

Luckily, most bears prefer to work in private and do this when people are not in their cabins. Of course, the odd bear that doesn't care whether you are home or not can often leave you running for your gun and then to the door in your long underwear...or less!

Polar Bear Research

Much of what we know about polar bears is the result of research conducted in the Churchill area. As part of a long-term study with over thirty years of continuous data, the Canadian Wildlife Service captures and studies bears along western Hudson Bay. They have most recently complete a three year mark recapture study indicating a marked decline in the western Hudson Bay population.

As part of this study, researchers locate polar bears from the air, traveling by helicopter along the coast of Hudson Bay, often within the boundaries of Wapusk National Park. Once a polar bear is spotted, researchers assess the location and the potential risk to the bear. Provided the bear is not close to water or another bear, the helicopter approaches. The vast majority of bears will try to get away; a few, however, have been known to turn and even take a swipe at the incoming researchers.

The pilot then attempts to position the helicopter almost directly above the bear. Researchers load a dart with Telazol – the drug used to immobilize bears - and try to place the dart in a spot between the neck and shoulders. This is one of the few spots on a polar bear where the fat layer is thin and the drug will be released directly into muscle. Once in the muscle it will circulate much more quickly than it would through fat tissue.

Once darted, the bear will stagger and stop, eventually sitting and then lying down. Once its head and neck are relaxed, the researchers land and approach. The bear is then placed in what is called a 'sternal recumbent position', which is simply lying on its stomach with all four legs spread out. This position places the least strain on the bear while the researchers are working.

After heart rate, breathing and body temperature have been recorded, the bear is checked for identifying tattoos and ear tags. Previously handled bears will have a tattoo on the inside of its lip and little white ear tags. Existing tattoos or ear tags are referred to the researcher's fieldbook in which all handled bear's histories are recorded. If the bear has not been handled before, it is recorded and given a unique number as well as an ear tag and tattoo. Each polar bear throughout the world has a code, such as X4040. Sometimes referred to as the 'x-files', all bears originally tagged in Canada begin with the letter X.

Measurements of length, girth, head length and head width are taken to determine the overall health of the polar bear. Researchers will also pull a tooth to determine the age of the bear. The tooth is one of the small premolar teeth right behind the canines, for which there is no known use. Back at the lab, the tooth is sectioned and the lines are counted, similar to counting rings on a tree. In polar bears, each line represents one year of age.

Finally, a small circle of dye is put on the back of each animal in order that it is not captured in the same season. This mark lasts four to five weeks and some bears still sport this mark during Churchill's bear season. After marking the bear, researchers ensure that there are no threatening bears in the area while their bear regains consciousness before boarding the helicopter to head off in search of another 'x-file'.

The Future

Late in 2005, the Canadian Wildlife Service released the preliminary results of their latest mark-recapture population study for western Hudson Bay. Their findings indicated a new estimate of approximately 1000 bears, a decline of over 20% from the last inventory completed in the mid-1990s.

According to Canadian Wildlife Service data, there has also been a general decline in the body condition of these bears since the early 1980s. Basically what this means is that twenty years ago, it was easier for polar bears to build up their fat reserves before coming ashore for the summer.

While this is not readily apparent in Churchill's polar bears, this trend will first affect the periphery of the western Hudson Bay population: the very old and the very young. It will become increasingly tougher for these bears to compete for food with the healthy part of the population leading to increased mortality.

Of course, climate models predict a significant decline in ice cover on Hudson Bay over the next twenty years. Without ice as their hunting platform, the age of the bear will not matter when it comes to mortality.

An extended season on shore also means that bear encounters are on the increase. A good example of this was the 2003 season in which the bears came on shore by late June and stayed until early December. Polar Bear Alert recorded a total of 176 bears handled, representing 138 individual bears (some being handled more than once). The vast majority of these bears, about 80%, were encountered in Zone 2, stretching from the the eastern edge of town to just past the Churchill dump.

However, in 2005, the world-renowned Churchill garbage dump was finally closed and a recycling/waste transfer station was established at L5, a former military building located near the airport. This is a positive move for both the bears and the community but will leave many of the return visitors to the garbage dump without a 'regular hangout'. Whether these bears venture into town or into cabins or just adapt and wait, remains to be seen. Regardless, with climate change increasing the bears' on shore season, Churchill's Polar Bear Alert program looks to be quite busy for the years to come.

To the north, the Inuit are increasingly seeing bears in their communities and on the land. Using traditional knowledge as a baseline, they have increased their population estimate for western Hudson Bay to 1,400. Following this, they have also increased their hunting quotas not only in western Hudson Bay but throughout much of the arctic, as well.

With two widely differing population estimates and widely differing management views, the next few years will be critical for this population. As well, concerns about climate change, global pollution and local encroachment, all point to an uncertain future for the polar bears of Churchill.

Polar Bear Who's Who

Subadults

- These are slender, smaller bears with 'longish' features. Neither their head nor their rump has filled out.
- From the ages of three to five, it is difficult to tell between the sexes. While males may be larger, it is best to look for the urine stain on the female's back legs.
- Most active bears, they often wander seemingly aimlessly, getting into trouble as they go. However, with less muscle and fat stores, they can sprint quickly, easily outrunning larger bears.
- May team up to hunt, scavenge and defend themselves. Young bears have been witnessed pairing up to drive off older, much larger bears.
- In some years, up to 40% of Churchill's cubs went off on their own at about 1.5 years old, other years the vast majority stay in the family until over two years of age.

Seniors

- Polar bears tend to decline in health after the age of fifteen years old. Males usually will not survive past twenty, while females seldom pass thirty.
- They look recognizably haggard. Unable to hunt effectively or defend their kills, their skin hangs on their bones, giving them an 'angular' look. This is most noticeable at their shoulder and hind quarter.
- Older bears command respect, their aggression tolerated by more dominant bears…for a while.
- Extremely dangerous bears, they may be in constant pain due to arthiritis, old injuries, abessed teeth or atrophying muscles.
- They tend to have a large number of scars or even major injuries, ranging from broken jaws to missing ears.
- One of the bears most likely to vocalize, occasionally with a loud, unearthly roar.

Males	**Females**

- A fully grown male polar bear is just big. They can measure over four metres (12'+) standing on their hind legs.
- There is a wide range in size, however. Adult males can be as small as 300kg (660 lbs). The largest male recorded in the Hudson Bay area was in excess of 650 kg (1,430 lbs).
- Though sexually mature by age five, male polar bears are not fully grown until age eight or nine.
- Males have large, heavily muscled necks, wider than their head. For this reason, you will never see a male bear with a radio collar.
- Males have a few long guard hairs hanging down from that 'special place'.
- Adult males often have scarring on their face, neck and, sometimes, rump. Exposing their black skin, these scars are the easiest way to identify individual bears.

- Females are visibly smaller than males, about 2/3 of a full grown male.
- Females range in weight from 150 to 250 kg (330-550 lbs). The largest adult females are close in size to the smallest adult males.
- They are generally more 'streamlined' and less 'massive'. Older female bears will, however, have a wide, flat forehead.
- Lone females are fairly common in the Gordon Point area and lend to some of the best viewing opportunities. Many times, they will venture along the coast, hunting for seals.
- They are fairly long-lived for bears, many reaching up to 25-30 years old in the wild. The oldest recorded bear in the wild was 33 years; in captivity: 41 years old.
- Again, an easy way to discern that it is a female bear is to look for the urine stain on their rump.

Bear Facts:
Bears of Western Hudson Bay

Size: Adult males approximately 2.5 metres (7.5') in length. At shoulder height (on all four legs). they can be up to 1.5 metres (4.5') and may reach up to 4 metres (12'+), standing on their hind legs.

Weight: Adult males can weigh as little as 300 kg to 800+ kg (660-1760 lbs). Most however range between 400-600 kg (880-1320 lbs). The largest male weight recorded was 654 kg, bears larger than this are too big for the scale. Their weight is estimated through measurements of girth and length.

Smaller than males, females commonly weigh in at 150 to 250 kg (330-550 lbs). Pregnant females, however, may reach in excess of 400 kg (880 lbs) prior to denning.

Maturity: Male polar bears reach their full size usually between the ages of 8-10 years, females by 5-6 years. Sexual maturity most commonly occurs around age five.

Longevity: In the wild, males may live to about 25 years of age, females into their late twenties or early thirties.

Diet: Predominantly ringed seal (usually seals one year of age or younger) but, depending on ice conditions, harbour and bearded seals are also consumed in Hudson Bay although to a lesser extent. They are also opportunistic hunters and scavengers and may graze on sedges, grasses or berries in the summer.

Reproduction: Mating occurs in April and May with pregnancy initiating in mid-September or early October. Cubs are born in early to mid-December (possibly as early as mid-November). Females must have at 200 kg (440 lbs) of fat reserves for implantation to occur in late September. Most common litter size is two, followed by litters of single cubs; triplets are rare.

Physical Adaptations

Nose - Often described as a 'Roman' profile, they have a very sleek look. Their sense of smell is at least twenty times stronger than human's with recent observations indicating that bears may be able to identify scents up to 100 kilometres (60 miles) away!

Neck - Their neck is long and agile; an adaptation to reaching down between cracks in the sea ice.

Legs – All bears are pigeon-toed with their front legs seemingly bow-legged. Again, this is an adaptation for hunting, in which they use their front paws to swipe at seals. They also swim by paddling with their front legs while their rear legs serve as a rudder.

Paws – Up to 12" (30cm) long, they are furred and covered in tiny bumps (called papillae) for increased traction. The skin is thick and in winter the paws are extremely furry making them highly resistant to cold.

Claws – Shorter, stronger than grizzlies but longer and sharper than black bears', they are designed for travel on sea ice and cutting flesh.

Tail and Ears – These extremities are smaller than other bears in order to reduce surface area and therefore heat loss. Small tail and ears result in the use of the neck and body movement as the main means of communications.

Teeth – Adapted for ripping and shearing meat as opposed to grinding, their teeth reflect their primarily carnivorous nature.

Eyes – They have brown, bloodshot eyes with similar eyesight to human but likely a bit farsighted. They also have a covering allowing for increased sensitivity at low light levels, probably tending towards the blue end of the spectrum.

Fat – By late spring, adult bears may have as much as 10cm (4") layer on their rump. This also aids in floatation while swimming but also means they easily overheat during the summer months.

Fur – They have two layers, oily guard hairs to quickly shed water and a woolly underlayer for insulation. Their underlayer is generally a creamy white or light yellow while their guard hairs have a hollow core, similar to expanded foam. Impurities, such as seal oil, in the guard hairs and the angle of sunlight contribute to the variation in colour through different seasons, especially apparent after the spring moult. These hollow hairs do not conduct heat or light to the skin as formerly hypothesized.

Skin – Their skin is entirely black, including their tongue. This is most likely an evolutionary holder over from their ancestor, the brown bear. Polar bears evolved along the same line as brown bears diverging only about 200,000 years ago.

Breath - Their breath quite often smells like ringed seals. Do not test this theory at home.

Source: The Polar Bear - Ursus maritimus: Biology, Management, and Conservation by Steven C. Amstrup

Suggested Reading

Here is a brief list of suggested reading about polar bears, Churchill and the arctic in general. All of these books have been utilized as a source and as inspiration for this handbook.

- A Naturalist's Guide to the Arctic by E.C. Pielou
- Bear: Celebration of Power & Beauty by Daniel Cox and Rebecca Grambo
- Bears: Monarchs of the Northern Wilderness by Wayne Lynch
- Churchill On Hudson Bay by Angus & Bernice MacIver
- Edge of the Arctic by Robert Taylor
- Encounters with Arctic Animals by Fred Bruemmer
- Journey to the Northern Sea by Samuel Hearne
- Polar Bears by Ian Stirling
- Polar Dance by Tom Mangelsen and Fred Bruemmer
- Tales from the Tundra by Glenn Hopfner
- The Arctic by Fred Bruemmer
- The World of the Polar Bear by Norbert Rosing

Bibliography

Scientific information in this book is based on the work of the following research scientists (listed in alphabetical order):

Steven Amstrup, Dennis Andriashek, Andrew Desrocher, Markus Dyck, John Iacozza, Charles Jonkel, Nick Lunn, Nils Oritslund, Susan Poleschuk, Malcolm Ramsay, Evan Richardson, Scott Schliebe, Peter Scott, Ian Stirling, Paul Watts.

It is thanks to the work of these individuals and many more that we enjoy such an extensive knowledge and respect for this top predator and symbol of the arctic.

A full bibliography and list of suggested reading can be found online at www.polarbearalley.com

Acknowledgements

This book is the result of several years of contact with Churchill's polar bears both guiding polar bear tours and living in Churchill. The bulk of my knowledge of bears was variably gained at the 'shop' (a.k.a. the Tundra Buggy garage) or Northern Nights Lounge. This is where Len Smith, the original owner of Tundra Buggy Tours, and several of the drivers would retire to after a 'hard day's drive' on the tundra. Their stories and their true appreciation for polar bears is the real inspiration for this book.

Of course, the bears themselves are responsible for my growing fascination and respect for this incredible creature. Each year, they offer something new and are truly an animal that inspires.

Over the next few years, I will be compiling a collection of stories about climate change and polar bears from a northern perspective, plus the odd reflection on cabin renovations, outdoor martini bars and other things arctic. Learn more about this collection at:

www.polarbearalley.com

Additional photographs contributed by:

Northern Soul
Wilderness Canoe Adventures

Paddle with beluga whales in Churchill,
Relive the fur trade along the Hayes,
Invigorate your spirit on the Bloodvein

www.northernsoul.ca

POLAR BEARS INTERNATIONAL

'Conservation through Research and Education'

www.polarbearsinternational.org

- Notes -

- Notes -

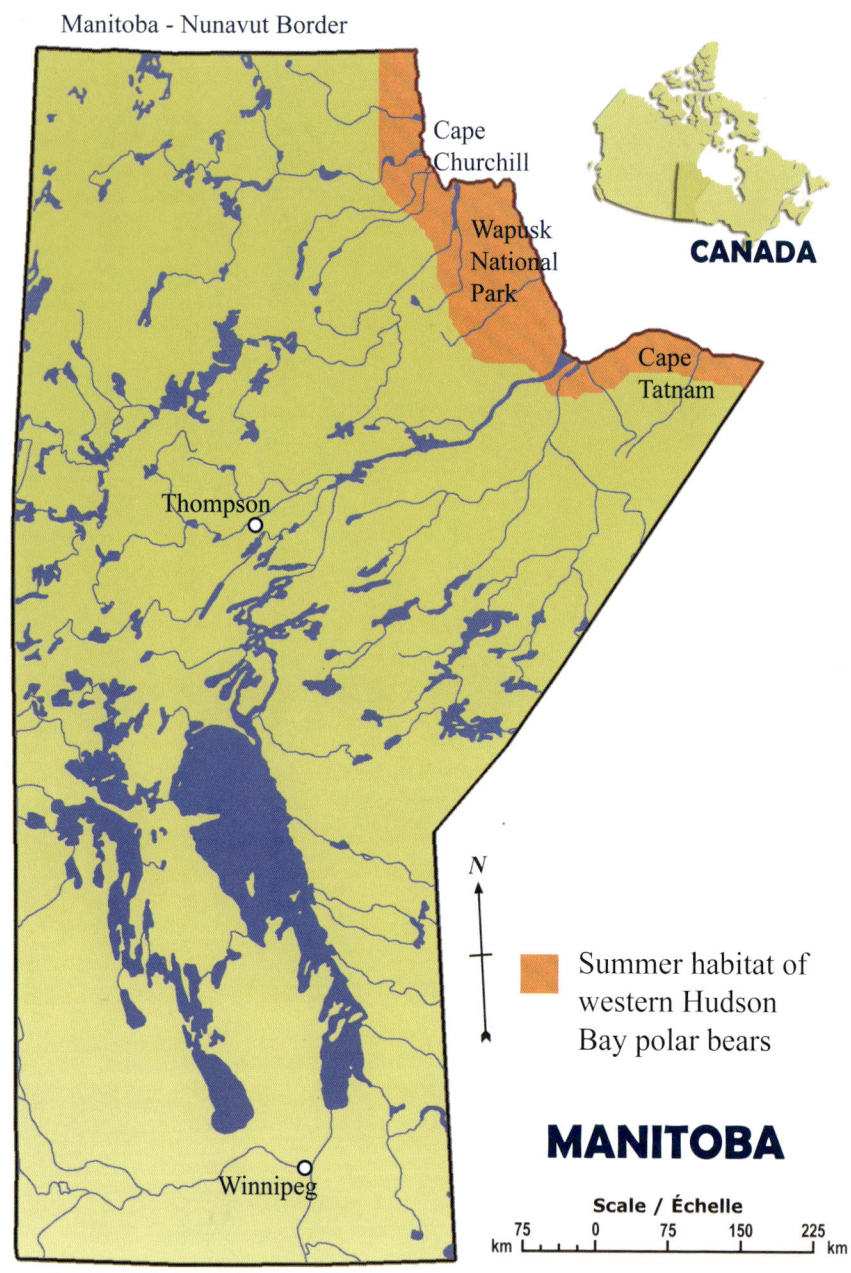